The
Connell Short Guide
to
Henrik Ibsen's

———————

A Doll's House

———————

by
Kirsten Shepherd-Barr

Contents

Introduction

Do boys play with dolls?

Not in provincial Norway in 1879. Not even today–unless the dolls are superhero figures.

By using the word "doll" Ibsen's play calls attention immediately to girls. Sometimes people argue that *A Doll's House* is not concerned with the plight of women, but is about the universal need to find self-fulfilment in life. They often point to a statement Ibsen made late in his career about not being a feminist. "I am not a member of the Women's Right League," he said rather ungraciously in a speech to the Norwegian League of Women's Rights who were giving him a banquet to celebrate his seventieth birthday. "I thank you for the toast, but must disclaim the honour of having consciously worked for the women's rights movement." He explained that his emphasis was on art and poetry, not "propaganda." The key word in Ibsen's speech is "consciously." He called his play *A Doll's House* because he was focusing on gender; he made his main character a woman so that he could expose a deep societal problem, namely how women are treated like dolls, or playthings, by the patriarchal society. But he did not write a prescription and solve a problem; he simply posed a question in the form of a play. What are women in contemporary life supposed to do; how can they live in a male-dominated world?

By the time a small, plucky group in England put on the play in a dingy theatre in London in 1889, *A Doll's House* had already become a sensation in most of Europe. It has since become one of the most written-about and performed plays in the world. The societal problems it exposed in 1879 when it was first published and performed have by no means gone away or been fully resolved. Clearly, this is a play that dissects conventional bourgeois society, exposing its rigidity and the constraints it places upon character and on each individual life. There is another very prominent issue at stake too, and that is the relationship between parents and their children. But even more significantly, the dramatic innovations the play presented have left a long legacy on modern drama in terms of how plays are written, beginning with a very basic element: the plot.

A summary of the plot

Norway, 1870s. A young woman's husband is suddenly taken gravely ill, and the doctor's advice is to go south to a warmer climate for as long as it takes for him to get well. The woman knows they can't afford it, but she wants to save her husband's life, so she thinks she will ask her father for help. But her father dies before she can ask him, so out of desperation she forges her father's signature so that she can borrow money from a shady lender named Krogstad with her father as guarantor for the loan. The couple goes to Italy, the husband recovers fully and returns to become head of the local bank.

Nice story; very dramatic. That would certainly make a great play. But this doesn't describe the plot of *A Doll's House*: all of this has happened many years earlier, and when the curtain rises we only see its aftermath. Ibsen starts his play where other playwrights of the time would have ended theirs. Everything seems fine at the start of A Doll's House: Torvald is settling in as bank director; Nora is happily getting ready for Christmas, decorating the tree in their living room, humming a little tune. The two of them flirt a bit, Torvald calling her his little lark and squirrel and saying how satisfied he is to be in good health, with a lovely wife and family and a successful career. Then an unexpected visitor arrives: Nora's old school friend, Mrs Linde, who has come to ask for a job from Torvald, because she is a widow with no money or children who has had to take care of her sick mother and her brothers, leaving her sobered and haggard by comparison with the pretty, vibrant Nora, happy mother of three and wife of prosperous bank manager.

As so often in Ibsen's plays, a knock on the door in the midst of seeming domestic bliss sets in motion of series of catastrophic events. This time it is Krogstad: he used to work with Torvald but got in trouble for embezzling funds, went to prison, and turned loan shark. He is the one who, unbeknownst to Torvald, lent Nora the money that allowed the family to go to Italy on the trip that saved Torvald's life. Nora is startled to see Krogstad, thinking he is here to demand repayment more quickly than they had agreed; but he has come to ask Torvald for a job. Torvald is above hiring someone with a shady past.

On his way out, Krogstad is surprised to see Mrs Linde, his old flame. Indeed, the house is brimming with visitors; the old family friend of the Helmers, Dr Rank, comes next, and reveals that he is dying of a mysterious hereditary illness that we can only surmise is syphilis, though no one seems to take much notice. He is secretly in love with Nora and when, later in the play, she is desperate for someone to turn to for the money to pay Krogstad back and clear herself of her debt — since Krogstad threatens to tell Torvald about the forged signature in retaliation for being snubbed by Torvald — she nearly asks Dr Rank but before she can, he reveals his love for her and she turns away, feeling that to ask him for money when she knows his true feelings would be wrong. Nora grows increasingly desperate as she tries to prevent Torvald learning the truth. In one stunning scene, she rehearses a feverish Sicilian dance called the

tarantella which she will dance in peasant costume at a party the Helmers are throwing. The passion and hysteria she shows through her dance inflame Torvald's desire and, when they are alone, he confides that at parties he pictures her across the room as a virgin whom he can't wait to seduce. He says all of this to Nora while she is offstage, in the next room, and he is lying on their bed waiting for her; she has gone to "throw off her masquerade costume" but little does he suspect it is to be substituted for a street dress and that she is about to leave him for good. They spend the final scene of the play discussing their relationship, Nora calmly and coolly explaining that seeing Torvald condemn her for a deed she did out of love for him and that harmed no one else made her realize he was not prepared to support her, to take her side. He is appalled: "no man sacrifices his honor for the one he loves!" She retorts: "Millions of women have done so." Nora says their marriage is not a true partnership because she has simply passed from her father's hands to her husband's and is merely his plaything; she has never had a proper education in anything and must start from scratch, on her own. He tries desperately to understand and first commands and then tearfully begs her to stay. She is resolute; and as she leaves, we hear the door slam and we see Torvald alone on stage, only just beginning to comprehend her viewpoint.

What the critics said

Early critics of Ibsen had strong views on the play. On one extreme was George Bernard Shaw, who adored Ibsen and emulated him. Shaw's lectures on "The Quintessence of Ibsenism" in 1890 were published under that title and became widely read; they still give great insight into not just a fellow playwright's "take" on Ibsen but, more revealingly, Shaw's own views on theatre (it was quickly dubbed "the quintessence of Shavianism"). On the other extreme was August Strindberg, the Swedish playwright and younger rival of Ibsen, who was notoriously misogynistic and loathed Ibsen's feminism. His 3-act drama *Sir Bengt's Wife* (1882) put the wife firmly back in her place, an idea he developed further in his comedy *Marauders* (1886) which showed the husband's mental superiority to the wife. As Egil Törnqvist notes, the title Marauders "refers to the pseudo-Darwinian idea that woman, after thousands of years of male development, mistakenly believes that she has the right to come marauding into his territory."

One of Ibsen's biographers, Michael Meyer, found Nora "an irrational and frivolous narcissist," a view in line with readers who see her as hysterical, vain, abnormal, egotistical, and selfish (all terms used by critics in recent years, as Templeton points out in her book Ibsen's Women).

More recently, Erroll Durbach insists on a reading of Nora as Everyman, a universalism that Joan Templeton entirely refutes when she calls the play "Ibsen's most explicit treatment of the woman question." In short, there is a plethora of views on Nora and on the play more generally.

Writing about one of Ibsen's later plays, *The Master Builder* (1893), Toril Moi suggests that it asks a fundamental existential question: "is it possible to find meaning in life when one feels that one's future is shrinking with every day that passes?" This question is not just a concern of late Ibsen but already lies at the heart of *A Doll's House*. It helps to explain the urgency with which Nora must leave; why she can't put off her departure but must make the most of every day that is passing, and try to offset all the wasted days already gone before she came to her great realization about the need to go out into the world and find out who she really is. This problem is not new to Ibsen: already in *Peer Gynt* (1867) he satirizes the character who is not wholly and committedly himself but is only partially self-realized, only himself "enough." In that play's climactic scene, Peer peels an onion looking for the core that lies beneath all the layers, only to discover that an onion has no core. Nora's departure is necessary for her to discover her true self and, if there is none, to create one, once she has discarded the empty layers of the self that she

inherited and adopted unthinkingly from the
society around her.

"The Modern Tragedy"

There are no dead bodies littering the stage at the
end of *A Doll's House*, as in the classics of Western
drama that have provided a template for what we
call tragedy, such as *Hamlet, King Lear, Oedipus
Rex*. But Ibsen self-consciously called it that: in
his "Notes to the Modern Tragedy," his
preliminary jottings as he began work on the play,
Ibsen challenges this age-old model of tragedy by
bringing it up to date and saying that you don't
need to have heaps of corpses on stage (or indeed
death at all) in order to have a tragedy—though in
later plays, from *The Wild Duck* onwards, he gives
us plenty of dead bodies at the end. Ibsen's notes
begin: "There are two laws: one for men, another,
entirely different, for women." He's not just talking
about the law in a legal sense, but in a natural
sense as well; how men and women are built
differently (both physically and spiritually) yet
women are forced to conform to a system that only
recognizes masculine modes of being and thinking.
"A woman cannot be herself in contemporary
society; it is an exclusively male society with laws
drafted by men and with counsel and judges who
judge feminine conduct from the male point of

view." By giving his play the subtitle "a modern tragedy" Ibsen is announcing that this unacknowledged but fundamental difference between men and women, with the resulting impoverishment of women's lives, is the single greatest tragedy of contemporary life. He is also consciously following the injunction of the influential Danish critic Georg Brandes that modern literature should "submit problems to debate," as he put it in a lecture in 1871 that reverberated throughout Scandinavia's artistic and intellectual circles. As the late eminent Ibsen scholar and translator James McFarlane puts it, the play's drama erupts when a woman's "natural instincts are brought into conflict with the notions of authority she has grown up with."

Ibsen actually got his idea for the play from real life. Nora Helmer was modelled on a young woman of Ibsen's acquaintance, Laura Kieler, whose painful story he adapted to his creative needs. She was an aspiring writer who confided in Ibsen that when her husband developed tuberculosis, she secretly borrowed money in order to take him as the doctors advised to a warmer climate; but, pressured by her creditors, she ended up committing forgery in order to get more money. When her husband discovered her crime, he demanded a divorce and he took her children away from her. She ended up in a mental asylum for a period. At the time, everyone in their circle knew instantly that Ibsen's play was based on her story, and it caused Laura Kieler deep distress that this tragic and deeply personal situation was revealed which she had told Ibsen in complete confidence. It is indeed a cruel irony that a play that seeks to remedy the exploitation of women should so ruthlessly exploit one unfortunate woman.

Ibsen and Feminism

Nevertheless, Ibsen dared to put on the stage an issue that was simmering away throughout the Victorian period. He helped to unleash the full force of the woman's movement and the widespread agitation for the vote. His articulation of the double standard, the "two laws," directly influenced fellow playwrights like Oscar Wilde who uses the phrase in his play *An Ideal Husband* (1893), and Shaw, whose plays and prefaces from the 1890s in particular explore the gender divide that Ibsen so powerfully articulated.

Ibsen's life-long interest in the plight of women can be found everywhere, in play after play, utterly refuting that speech he made in 1898 denying his interest in women's issues and which can be explained by his fear of being affiliated with any one particular group, whether feminist, Socialist, anarchist, or Symbolist; he wanted to be his own man. His work is, in a very real sense, one long meditation on women's issues. When someone asks you what *A Doll's House* is about, or *Ghosts*, or *The Lady from the Sea*, or *Rosmersholm,* or *Hedda Gabler*, you start by saying, "It's about a woman who..."

But Ibsen also wrote many plays that you would start out describing as, "It's about a man who...." Many of these have to do with men having to juggle family demands with all-consuming careers, particularly artists, as in *When We Dead Awaken* (1900), Ibsen's last word on this subject and a very agonizing, guilt-ridden self-portrait. How far, he seems to be asking, does devotion to one's calling and vocation pre-empt all other aspects of life, including family? He explored this in *Brand* (1865); he explored it in *The Master Builder* (1892); and again in *When We Dead Awaken,* plays that revolve around sacrifice and compromise.

They also show the pitfalls of a too-rigid commitment to idealism, the "all-or-nothing" mentality. Ibsen shows the need for such engrained, archaic masculine traits to be stripped away from modern men. Thus, a play like *A Doll's House* doesn't just point an accusing finger at men. It would never have had the staying power that it has if it just did that. Instead, he shows how both men and women unconsciously play roles they seem to be expected to play: the obedient wife, the authoritative husband, the loving mother, the distant father, and so on. *A Doll's House* is ultimately about how all of us play roles in life, usually unconsciously and therefore unquestioningly—a theme that Italian playwright Luigi Pirandello explored in his modernist dramas several decades later.

Nora is a sexual object. Her husband sees her constantly in a sexual light, confiding to her after the party at which she so enticingly danced the tarantella that he imagines her as his young bride, "that we are just leaving our wedding, that I am taking you to our new home for the first time...to be alone with you for the first time...quite alone with your young and trembling loveliness!" He needs to turn back time and make her a virgin again, fantasizing about her virginity and erasing the fact that she is a sexually mature woman who has had three children with him. The "trembling" is especially revealing: Ibsen was fully aware of the growing discourse, particularly in frank novels by his contemporaries in Scandinavia, around the "suffer and be still" predicament of young women who were not told what to expect on their wedding night, but kept in sexual ignorance only to become traumatized by their painful initiation. What is Ibsen suggesting about men's expectations of, and attitudes toward, women? Nora is one of a long line of female characters Ibsen created who are older and already mothers and wives with a history and with sexual experience. He seems to be saying that this is when women get interesting, once the challenges of post-marital life kick in and collide with their own growth. Yet most well-made plays of the age focused on young, inexperienced ingénues and ended with marriage, rather than showing what happens once the wedding is over.

Not only Torvald but Dr Rank sexualized Nora. He confides—devastatingly for Nora—that he is in love with her in their scene with the silk stockings; this scene shocked audiences and critics at the time with its allusion to the naked female body, even if only the legs. She had depended on him as a friend, the one man in her life who didn't seem to need to see her in a sexual way; and she was just about to ask him for financial help precisely because it wouldn't involve anything sexual. Now, this revelation of his love for her shuts down her one remaining avenue of help.

Questioning Heroes and Villians

Dr Rank is a strange character: a figure of death, as he confides that he is doomed by hereditary disease and will shortly die, to be signalled, he reveals, by leaving a black-edged calling card. He is a doctor who can diagnose but cannot cure—one of several in Ibsen's dramas, they can only stand helplessly by as disease and death take hold. Dr Rank is often referred to as the play's raisonneur; this was a stock character in the well-made play (and earlier, for example in Moliere's dramas). But is he really the voice of reason? In earlier drafts to *A Doll's House*, he is downright scary and far from reasonable, fanatically advocating eugenics in order to cleanse society of the unfit. In the final version, his presence, so near death, is ghostly, a sickly foil to the vitality of Nora and her children.

The key thing about *A Doll's House* is that its "tragedy of modern life" is not just Nora's tragedy, but Torvald's, Krogstad's, and Dr Rank's, too; not just women's but men's. The play seems to be asking what kinds of models we have before us as we shape ourselves into adults? Nora says she has to start from scratch and find her own models because she's had none. But perhaps even more damaging are the bad models that the men have had in their lives. Far from being villains, the male characters in the play are, like Nora, simply replicating patterns of behaviour that have persisted through most of history.

Indeed, one of Ibsen's great innovations was to blur the lines between heroes and villains, showing how hard it is to distinguish between the two and how human character is made up of both sides. Yes, Torvald is annoying; he bosses Nora around, condescendingly calls her his "little squirrel" and "lark" and other demeaning pet names and "tut-tuts" all the time as he finds her wanting in so many ways. He treats her like a child and like his plaything. But Ibsen shows that in the end he is as much a victim of society's upbringing as she is—the play's ending suggests that he too will have to unlearn everything he's ever learned about being a man, especially in his understanding of women. It's moving to see him struggle throughout that final discussion scene, always just a step behind Nora but desperate to fix their problems. He assumes the hysterical female role while she becomes the calm, collected, masterful man.

Meanwhile, Krogstad seems on the surface to be the stereotypical villain. A shady character with a dodgy past, he has done time in prison for embezzlement and he is a loan shark. He shows little mercy when Nora pleads for more time to repay the loan, and seems in fact to enjoy her discomfort. But he has been treated badly too: Torvald turned his back on Krogstad just when he needed him most. What kinds of models has he had to follow? Thus Ibsen sets up character foils: Nora and Mrs Linde, Torvald and Krogstad, to complicate and deepen the play's treatment of gender. We are constantly weighing one against the other.

What makes it even harder to dislike Krogstad is his genuine soft spot for Mrs Linde. Their union in the end humanizes him. While Mrs Linde acts as a foil for Nora and a rather obvious tool for the exposition of the play in the opening scenes when Nora has to explain to her—and hence to the audience—everything that has happened in the past, there is much more to her character than being a mere device. It is Mrs. Linde who prompts Nora to reveal her big secret by saying dismissively that Nora is immature and child-like: Nora bristles and to set Mrs Linde straight she tells all about the loan, about working hard and doing without fine new clothes in order to pay it off. Mrs Linde also serves as a reminder to the audience of how few alternatives there are for women to support themselves and still be "respectable." But Mrs Linde also has a fully developed character of her own. Her union with Krogstad is not just for convenience but because she recognizes in him a fellow "shipwrecked soul."

The quiet heroism of the female characters is not just admirable; it also deftly casts Torvald's manly pronouncements in a foolish and melodramatic light. "You know, Nora...many's the time I wish you were threatened by some terrible danger so I could risk everything, body and soul, for your sake." Hardly swept off her feet by this, Nora's reaction is to say, "firmly and decisively": "Now you must read your letters." She and the audience know that what he imagines himself heroically doing is what she quietly did for him all those years ago.

FIVE FACTS ABOUT
Henrik Ibsen and *A Doll's House*

1.

In 2001, the autographed manuscripts of *A Doll's House* were placed on the Memory of the World Register in recognition of their historical value.

2.

Ibsen's son, Sigurd, served as the Prime Minister of Norway between 1903 and 1905.

3.

2006 marked the 100th anniversary of Ibsen's death and was known as 'Ibsen Year' in several countries. Events including an opening ceremony, television programmes and live performances celebrated the life of the playwright.

4.

Ibsen was nominated for the Nobel Prize in Literature in 1902, 1903 and 1904. He didn't win as the judges deemed his work to be too realistic.

5.

In 1995, an asteroid was named after Ibsen in honour of his work.

Opposite: Christopher Eccleston as Neil Kelman (based on Krogastad) and Gillian Anderson as Nora in the 2009 production of A Doll's House at the Donmar Warehouse in London

A peculiar title

The title by which most of the world knows the play is in fact a mistranslation. Ibsen didn't call the play "A Doll's House"; he called it "A Doll Home." This is something very different, and very strange; when have we ever used such a term? What is a "doll home"? It is a shame that the title always gets translated as "A Doll's House," because that is a cliché; in the same way, Ibsen calls one of his later plays "The Lady from the Sea," rather than the more cliché term "The Mermaid." He is using a technique that Modernist writers would call "estrangement," or alienation: making strange the familiar, or in other words, using a term that sounds very like something we know well but isn't quite the same. It makes us think afresh about our assumptions of what a "doll's house" or a "mermaid" really is. *A Doll's House* suggests a little girl's plaything. "A Doll Home" suggests something much more sinister: how that idea of a girl playing with dolls has spread beyond the neat confines of a little house, to pervade the real home—the real life of the characters, and of every woman. And the tragedy is that Nora is living as a doll in her own home and passing that role on, unthinkingly, to her own children.

But many productions choose not to show real children on stage, merely to allude to them. Ibsen's script is written in such as way that this is entirely possible, for example having the hide-and-seek game in Act I played entirely without them, with Nora simply alone and "hiding" on stage and speaking to them as if they are in nearby rooms that we can't see. This can send a powerful message, making a thematic point (and saving money on child actors) by suggesting through their absence that Nora is already gone from their lives.

Conversely, Ibsen does require the presence of the nursemaid, and for good reason: the audience needs to be made fully aware that Nora's departure will not actually ruin the children's lives but, chillingly, the women who have nursed Nora will step in and nurse her children once she's gone; and she knows this. They represent yet another point on the female spectrum of the play, with its different stages of female emancipation—Mrs Linde arguably the most advanced at the play's start, Nora emergent and finally fully emancipated by the end (at least in gesture), and the maid and the nanny unquestioningly subservient and poised to replicate the same behavioural patterns Nora is trying to break.

How plausible is Nora's Transformation?

One of the earliest, and most egregious, English stage adaptations *A Doll's House* was called *Breaking a Butterfly* (1882). This travesty, featuring a melodramatic and hysterical Flora (nicknamed Flossie) growing excessively distraught and agitated throughout the play, illustrates how unacceptable Ibsen's Nora was seen to be by the male adaptors (Henry Arthur Jones and Henry Herman, both seasoned playwrights). This version shows how far Ibsen had gone from 19th-century melodrama, with its heightened emotion, its stock characters, and its frequent reliance on deus ex machina to end the play in a speedy—though utterly contrived—manner. It also foregrounds the idea of Nora as a butterfly.

A butterfly appears to transform instantaneously from immature to fully developed being, breaking out of its chrysalis, spreading its wings, and flying away. But it has been maturing inside its cocoon in a process hidden from the outside world. Ibsen's Nora is no butterfly—she doesn't go suddenly from girl to woman—but he does show her character developing incrementally so that when she "transforms" it is not sudden and shocking, but is the logical result of a series of hints that has been carefully planted in the text since the very first moments, when we see Nora hiding the macaroons and lying to Torvald about them. She confides in Mrs Linde about her secret manuscript copying and the fact that she enjoyed such seemingly dull work, and she also shows unexpected canniness in recognizing that her only power over Torvald lies in her youthful prettiness; once that is gone, she will lose her hold. With Mrs

Linde she also shows her enjoyment of swearing and being naughty.

Another set of clues is in the metaphor of masking that Ibsen scatters throughout the play, riffing on the idea of costuming, masquerade, pretence and artifice—a metatheatrical allusion, since this is a play about the damage done by playing roles. In Act I, Torvald denounces Krogstad as a liar, and liars are always dissembling; they can never "drop the mask," not even with their own wives and children. Even Dr Rank employs this masking metaphor when he takes his final leave: "at the next masquerade, I shall be invisible....There's a big black cloak..." —the cloak of death.

Yet earlier in the play, when he is alone with Nora and she playfully shows him her silk stockings, it is not artful flirtation and pretence but a core truth and essential trust that they share. The scene shows Nora's real self, free of societal pressures and able to relax, until that rare sense of liberation is shattered when Dr. Rank reveals that he loves her, thereby showing that he is no different from any other man attracted to her sexually. This enables Nora's nobility with him after his declaration of love.

Further clues to her gradual transformation are her enactment of melodramatic, hysterical gestures only to reject them or grow out of them: the tarantella dance and the momentary thought of suicide as a way out. These enable her to realize the importance of steeling herself and facing the inevitable rather than running away: she says "firmly and decisively," "now you must read your letters, Torvald."

All hell breaks loose when Torvald reads the letter, but he is the emotional one, not her; the firm, decisive tone stays with her throughout the final scene, her demeanor becomes "icily calm" and she remains absolutely in control for the duration, while Torvald switches roles to become the stereotypically hysterical "female." He even marvels at her "calm, collected manner" as she confesses that she no longer loves him and they watch their lives crumble. Indeed, from the start of the play to its close, Torvald is too rigid, always one step behind in his understanding of this idea of change; in Act II, for example, he is disappointed when he peeks at Nora's supposed costume for the party, as he had "expected some kind of marvellous transformation." This in itself is a proleptic signal of what momentous change will eventually come.

The final way in which Ibsen plants the transformative seed right from the start is in echoing certain ideas from the beginning of the play in a vastly different light near the end in order to show how deeply Nora has changed. For instance, in the opening moments of the play, she says: "Oh, I only wish I'd inherited a few more of Daddy's qualities." But by the end of the play she is rejecting this patriarchal inheritance entirely, saying that she has simply "passed out of Daddy's hands into yours [Torvald's]" with no innate ideas of her own.

The audience has to be alert to the clues Ibsen places for us. It's a new kind of playwriting, very subtle and pointedly anti-melodramatic. It requires as well a new kind of psychological awareness on the part of the actress—and this is exactly why so many actresses at the time loved Ibsen and rejoiced in his new roles for them. At last, there was depth and a backstory to female characters.

Rewriting the "well-made play"

The turning point in the play is not when Torvald discovers the letter. That may well be the climax in an old-fashioned style of play, full of bombast and excitement as the word "climax" would suggest. Ibsen gives us that moment but then provides an even more electrifying, intense climax: the moment when Nora says that she and Torvald need to talk, a discussion that culminates in that final slam of the door with which the play ends. Ibsen simply withholds the traditional resolution. Audiences were stunned to find the lights coming up when they were expecting the action to go on, with Nora returning and the two living happily ever after. This technique is similar to a detective story in that the on-stage action hinges on uncovering past events and secrets. Ibsen's technique is to spread the exposition of the play over its duration, rather than getting it over with in the first act, as in most dramas of the time. This is part of the "retrospective action" of the play.

Another new technique is that the play has almost no monologues or soliloquies (except for the moment when Nora is alone on stage and briefly contemplates throwing herself in the lake, but rejects that idea). The dialogue is spare, uses simple language, interruptions, hesitations, unfinished sentences—all of the things we do when we speak ordinary speech.

Finally there is Ibsen's use of place. In addition to blurring the distinction between "good" and "bad" characters by developing his characters more fully than had ever been done before on stage and making them psychologically real, Ibsen managed to be both local and universal in his use of setting. It continues to baffle critics that Ibsen can set play after play in a small Norwegian coastal town yet appeal to audiences all over the world, both in his own time and now. The setting of the plays has an astonishing flexibility despite the specificity of place.

Bernard Shaw claimed that *A Doll's House* "conquered Europe and founded a new school of dramatic art." As Egil Törnqvist notes in his superb consideration of the play, both statements are valid:

> The play has in fact by now conquered the world, and it has done so thanks to what Shaw termed 'the discussion,' the part for which, according to Ibsen himself, the whole play was written. However, what Shaw disregards is that it is the combination of the discussion and Nora's departure that does the trick. Nora not only talks, she also acts.

What will Nora do next?

The question of what Nora does next has never been resolved. Modern readers and audiences frequently wax eloquent about how wonderful it is for Nora that she has at last gained her freedom and independence. Yet she herself is clear-eyed about it. When Torvald asks if she will ever return to him, she says simply: "How should I know? I've no idea what I might turn out to be."

What are Nora's options upon exiting for good; what can she do, after all? She has never had a formal education and her upbringing in a comfortable family has not prepared her for any trade or occupation, just for being married. She can't be a governess, one of the few "respectable" jobs for a nineteenth-century woman. She can't teach anything because she has no education and no particular talents. So how will she support herself? Just about the only option available is prostitution. Unless, of course, the exit and slam of the door are just empty gestures and she comes back the next day, tail between legs.

That is what happened in some of the first German-language productions of the play. Directors of productions in Hamburg and Vienna wanted a "conciliatory" ending, while a famous actress preparing to take the role of Nora on tour refused to act the part unless the ending were changed, because she objected that she herself would never leave her children. At the time, there were no copyright laws protecting dramatists, so Ibsen reluctantly rewrote the ending of the play himself, rather than allow a second-rate hack writer to do it. Ibsen himself called this a "barbaric outrage." In the final moments of the play, Torvald drags Nora to the bedroom door to watch her children sleeping. He says softly, "Look, there they are asleep, peaceful and carefree. Tomorrow, when they wake up and call for their mother, they will be—motherless." Nora struggles with herself, lets her travelling bag fall, and "half sinks down by the door" as she says: "Oh, this is a sin against myself, but I cannot leave them." The "Alternative German Ending" makes a fascinating study in itself of the pressure of societal expectations on the playwright as well as the power of the role of Nora.

Plenty of sequels and spoofs were written at the time imagining what Nora did next because the play deliberately left this burning question unanswered. Bernard Shaw's *A Doll's House—And After* was one of the most prominent. Yet at the same time, Nora's exit is not a prescription, a "one size fits all" remedy for society's gender imbalance. Ibsen sets the precedent that so many subsequent dramatists follow: they pose questions, but don't provide answers. Theatre is particularly good at doing this because it generally lacks a narrator, that guiding voice telling us gently what we should think. This is why the lines in the final discussion scene are so famous, and so important:

> *Torvald: This is outrageous! You are betraying your most sacred duty!*
> *Nora: And what do you consider to be my most sacred duty?*
> *Torvald: Does it take me to tell you that? Isn't it your duty to your husband and your children?*
> *Nora: I have another duty equally sacred.*
> *Torvald: You have not. What duty might that be?*
> *Nora: My duty to myself.*

But there is no grand declamation here; Ibsen's stage directions call for a calm though serious tone, no histrionics, no melodrama. This is a private discussion we are witnessing, as if we are the invisible "fourth wall" of the room; it makes us more like voyeurs than audience members at a play. We sit there watching the breakdown of a marriage and then get up and leave, without any resolution or closure as we might expect. The closing of the door is *the* closure.

The power of illusions

When Nora announces that she is taking off her masquerade costume, she is saying that she's finished with performing a role, which is what women have to do to exist in society. This is thrilling stuff; she is a fearless truth-teller, a crusader willing to brave a hostile world for the sake of following through on her beliefs. Certainly, Nora will pay a huge price for her idealism. (Destitution? Prostitution? Humiliation by being forced by circumstances to return to the home she has just triumphantly renounced?) Maybe living with self-delusion would have been better. Ibsen's next play, *Ghosts*, shows exactly that: a woman who does remain in an unhappy marriage, for the sake of maintaining an illusion. The consequences are even more devastating than anyone could imagine, making the ending of *A Doll's House* seem benign by comparison: as the curtain comes down the female protagonist, Mrs Alving, is standing next to her brain-dead, syphilitic son clutching a fatal dose of pills he had given her earlier and instructed her to administer should his disease worsen. Before the audience has a chance to see whether she will do it, the play ends.

Ghosts was so scandalous across Europe that when Ibsen's supporters applied to have it performed in Britain in 1890, the Lord Chamberlain refused to grant a license – so they formed the Independent Theatre Company, helping to launch a wave of such enterprises (the "little theatre" movement), where audiences could see new drama that was too controversial to be produced on the mainstream stage.

But Ibsen was always one step ahead of his readers and audiences. He was a contrarian: just when they thought they had him pinned down, he surprised them by going completely against what he had done before. *The Pillars of Society* (1877), *A Doll's House, Ghosts* (1880), and *An Enemy of the People* (1882) were his first four "social problem" plays, each driving home a message about how important it is to tell the truth, to expose falsehood and illusion. This idealism is exactly what he then turns around and satirises in *The Wild Duck* (1884), a play that shows the terrible consequences that can arise from exposing the truth, from removing the important "life-lie" that sustains and comforts us because we cannot face the harsh light of truth and the shattering of our illusions. Arguably, the moral of *The Wild Duck* – that the truth can be dangerous – is exactly the opposite of the moral of *A Doll's House*.

FOUR MYTHS ABOUT
HENRIK IBSEN

1.
Queen Victoria and the Archbishop of Canterbury saw a production of *Ghosts* as part of her Jubilee celebrations in 1897.

It is simply unfathomable that this ever could have happened: why on earth would they go to see a play that had been refused a license by Her Majesty's government's own official censor, the Lord Chamberlain? It would be utterly inexplicable. And that is exactly why George Bernard Shaw thought it up—such a deliciously improbable event, so irresistible to imagine, presented in an 1897 article as if it were true. This bit of Shavian mischief was then incorrectly rendered as fact by Michael Egan in his book Ibsen: *The Critical Heritage*, a book that is one of the first sources anyone interested in Ibsen turns to. Tore Rem in his recent book on Ibsen (Henry Gibson) corrects the error but it lingers on, a booby-trap for new generations of Ibsen scholars and readers. It's important to correct this "factoid" because it gives a completely false sense of acceptance of Ibsen in England at a time when in fact his plays were still controversial and apt to shock— especially *Ghosts*, which was not granted a license until 1910.

2.
Ibsen is only interested in domestic drama.

Despite his reputation as a domestic dramatist, Ibsen is not exclusively focused on interiors. Though many of his plays are domestic dramas—*A Doll's House* is set entirely inside one house, for example—many of them are strikingly aware of nature and bring it on stage, whether literally or metaphorically. *Ghosts*, for instance, asks for a huge picture window showing the scene outside: endless rain and a gloomy view of the fjord. Avalanches occur in three of Ibsen's plays, and in *Peer Gynt* the lovely Solveig pursues Peer on skis, an entrance as memorable as that of the vibrant Hilde

Wangel hiking onto the stage in her mountain-walking costume and walking stick. The mermaid-like Ellida in *The Lady from the Sea* enters dripping wet from her swim in the fjord. Water, snow, mountains, the elements: nature is everywhere, and deeply influences Ibsen's characters. He was a pioneer in getting the drama to explore and stage how environment works on character.

3.
Ibsen was kicked out of Norway and went into exile.

In fact, he opted to live abroad, first in Italy and then in Germany for a total of 27 years until finally returning to Norway in 1891 at the age of sixty-three. He left to gain wider experience of life and exposure to new ideas, particularly the liberalism of Darwin, Mill, Brandes, and many other thinkers and writers of his time

4.
Ibsen is old-fashioned and boring.

For many decades of the 20th century there was a mistaken sense of Ibsen being "a fuddy-duddy old realist," as Toril Moi puts it. This says a lot about the shortness of memory, because at the time (1880s), realism was revolutionary, and naturalism even more so. As Moi argues, Ibsen's realism and naturalism have been misunderstood and have led to the assumption that he was only the precursor of modernism and not one of its foremost examples. In the theatre, realism and naturalism were key parts of modernism, not merely precursors to it, and Moi shows how integral these developments were to what became known as the modernist movement, particularly in the plays Ibsen wrote from 1880 onwards. The quintessential modernist, James Joyce, so revered Ibsen that he wrote his first substantial article on the playwright and, more importantly, tried to emulate his work in his own play, Exiles, written around 1915. Other modernist writers lauded Ibsen's work precisely for its mining of the psychological subconscious, rather than for his realist depictions of bourgeois life; German poet Rainer Maria Rilke admired Ibsen's "ever more desperate search for visible correlations of the inwardly seen," and Belgian Symbolist dramatist Maurice Maeterlinck sought to emulate Ibsen's "dialogue of the second degree," or the implied text beneath the spoken words.

A SHORT CHRONOLOGY

1828 20 March Henrik Ibsen is born

1850 *The Burial Mound,* Ibsen's first play

1879 Ibsen writes *A Doll's House*

1880 *A Doll's House* premieres in Stockholm

1884 *A Doll's House* opens in London

1906 23 May Ibsen dies

1917 Berthold Viertel directs a silent film adaptation

1973 Two film versions of *A Doll's House* are released, one directed by Joseph Losey and another by Patrick Garland

2013 Carrie Cracknell directs a production at the Young Vic in London

FURTHER READING

Toril Moi, *Henrik Ibsen and the Birth of Modernism* (Oxford University Press, 2006)

Toril Moi, introduction to *Ibsen: The Master Builder and Other Plays*, ed. Tore Rem (Penguin 2014)

George Bernard Shaw, *The Quintessence of Ibsenism* (1891)

Kirsten Shepherd-Barr, *Ibsen and Early Modernist Theatre*, 1890-1900 (Greenwood Press, 1997)

Joan Templeton, *Ibsen's Women* (Cambridge University Press, 1997)

Egil Törnqvist, Ibsen: A Doll's House, Plays in Production series (Cambridge University Press, 1995)

Bibliography

Michael Egan, ed., *Ibsen: The Critical Heritage.* London, 1972.

Robert Ferguson, *Henrik Ibsen: A New Biography.* London: Richard Cohen, 1996.

Daniel Haakonsen, ed. *Contemporary Approaches to Ibsen.* Vols. I and II. Oslo: University of Oslo Press, 1966 and 1971.

James McFarlane, ed. and trans. *The Oxford Ibsen.* 7 vols. Oxford: Oxford University Press, 1970.

James McFarlane, ed. *The Cambridge Companion to Ibsen.* Cambridge: Cambridge University Press, 1994.

James McFarlane and Jens Arup, trans., *Henrik Ibsen: Four Major Plays.* Oxford University Press, 1981.

Frederick J. Marker and Lise Lone Marker. *Ibsen's Lively Art: A Performance Study of the Major Plays.* Cambridge: Cambridge University Press, 1989.

Michael Meyer. *Ibsen*. London: Rupert Hart-Davis, 1971.

Toril Moi. Henrik Ibsen and the Birth of Modernism: Art, Theatre, Philosophy. Oxford: Oxford University Press, 2006.

Elizabeth Robins, *Theatre and Friendship*. London: Jonathan Cape, 1932.

George Bernard Shaw, *The Quintessence of Ibsenism*. London, 1891.

Kirsten Shepherd-Barr. *Ibsen and Early Modernist Theatre, 1890-1900*. Westport, Conn.: Greenwood Press, 1997.

Evert Sprinchorn, ed. and trans., *Ibsen: Letters and Speeches*. New York: 1964.

Joan Templeton, *Ibsen's Women*. Cambridge, 2001.

Egil Törnqvist, *A Doll's House: Plays in Production* series, Cambridge, 1995.

Thomas F. Van Laan. "Generic Complexity in Ibsen's An Enemy of the People." Comparative Drama, 20 (Summer 1986), 2: 95-114.

Ibsen Studies — the leading journal devoted to Ibsen-related criticism — and Ibsen.net

Bjørn Hemmer's overview of Ibsen's career: http://www.mnc net/norway/Ibsen.htm

Notes

Notes

Notes

First published in 2016 by
Connell Guides
Artist House
35 Little Russell Street
London WC1A 2HH

10 9 8 7 6 5 4 3 2 1

Picture credits:
p.5 Public Domain image
p.19 © Donald Cooper/REX

A CIP catalogue record for this book is available from the British Library.
ISBN 978-1-911187-02-8

Design © Nathan Burton
Written by Kirsten Shepherd-Barr
Edited by Jolyon Connell

Assistant editors and typesetting by
Paul Woodward and Holly Bruce
Five Facts compiled by Holly Bruce

www.connellguides.com